First published in the United States by
Ideals Publishing Corporation
Nashville, Tennessee 37214

First published in Great Britain by
Methuen Children's Books
London, England

Printed in Hong Kong by Mandarin Offset

Library of Congress Cataloging-in-Publication Data is available upon request.
Library of Congress Card Catalog Number 90-4618

ISBN 0-8249-8440-4

# DAISY'S CHRISTMAS

## MARTIN WADDELL

pictures by
Jonathan Langley

IDEALS CHILDREN'S BOOKS

Daisy was a dreamer.

Every night in her comfy little bed,
she thought about what she would like to dream,
and then she went to sleep and dreamed it.

On Monday night, Daisy dreamed that she was a princess.

She married a prince and lived happily ever after.

In the morning, Mom asked, "What was your dream like?"

And Daisy said, "It was boring."

On Tuesday night, Daisy dreamed that
she went on a long, long journey.
She traveled to New York and Paris

and Egypt, where she rode on a camel.
Daisy didn't enjoy it; it was hot and sticky.
Mom asked, "Are you too hot tonight?"

On Wednesday night, Daisy built a Noah's ark.

Daisy was Noah, and she put all the animals inside her ark.

Dad asked, "What's going on here?"

And Daisy said, "It was only a dream."

Dad said, "Some dream!"

Daisy put all the animals back in their cabinet.

On Thursday night, Daisy dreamed that she was a clown.

She threw pies at the other clowns.
It was very funny. All the people cheered.

On Friday night, Daisy went to Mars.
She wore a blue space suit.

Mars was full of monsters.
Daisy didn't like that dream.

On Saturday night, Daisy had a shipwreck.
Everyone fell off the boat.

Mom said, "Upsy-Daisy."

On Sunday night, Daisy dreamed that it was Christmas,

but her dream . . .

wasn't a dream after all.

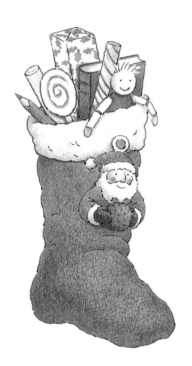